Plato: The Great Philosopher-Educator

Giants in the History of Education

David Diener, PhD

Series Editor: David Diener, PhD

Plato: The Great Philosopher-Educator

Version 1.1

ISBN: 978-1-60051-263-6

Cover & layout by Lenora Riley

Classical Academic Press
515 S. 32nd Street
Camp Hill, PA 17011
www.ClassicalAcademicPress.com

PGP.05.17

There is one element you could isolate in any account you give, and this is the correct formation of our feelings of pleasure and pain, which makes us hate what we ought to hate from first to last, and love what we ought to love. Call this "education," and I, at any rate, think you would be giving it its proper name.

—Plato, *Laws*

Table of Contents

ACKNOWLEDGMENTS

Throughout the process of writing and editing this book, I have benefited greatly from the valuable input offered by a number of people. Among those I particularly would like to thank are Marcus Foster, Glenn Hoshauer, Jeff Perkins, Jeremy Sturdivant, Brent Stevens, Jeanette Faulkner, "Skip" Cornelius Ferguson, and Steven Smith. I have appreciated deeply both my friendships with these scholar-educators as well as the intellectual community we have enjoyed together. Steve Turley and Louis Markos also offered helpful feedback on early drafts of this book, for which I am grateful. Over the years my understanding of Plato has grown both through the instruction of excellent teachers such as Bruce Benson, Barry Bull, Michael Morgan, and Paul Spade, and also through my interactions with numerous students in philosophy classes I have taught. I also owe an enormous debt of gratitude to my wife, Brooke, and our four children, who have supported my work on this book and made sacrifices for it.

Introduction

Any attempt to encapsulate Plato's thought regarding education is a daunting task. Plato's views are many and diverse, and throughout history innumerable analyses of his thought already have been made. The attention that has been paid to interpreting Plato, however, is certainly not undeserved. Plato is one of the principal founders of the Western intellectual tradition, and it is nearly impossible to examine the historical development of any academic topic without, knowingly or unknowingly, addressing Plato's views. As Alfred North Whitehead famously quipped, "The safest general characterization of the European philosophical tradition is that it consists of a series of footnotes to Plato."[1] Werner Jaeger similarly claims that, "To this day, the character of any philosophy is determined by the relation it bears to Plato. After him, every epoch of classical culture was marked by Platonic characteristics, however strangely altered they might be."[2]

Plato was one of the principal founders of the Western intellectual tradition, and it is nearly impossible to examine the historical development of any academic topic without, knowingly or unknowingly, addressing Plato's views.

1. Alfred North Whitehead, *Process and Reality: An Essay in Cosmology*, Gifford Lectures Delivered in the University of Edinburgh During the Session 1927–1928 (New York: Macmillan, 1929), 63.
2. Werner Jaeger, *Paideia: The Ideals of Greek Culture*, trans. Gilbert Highet (New York: Oxford University Press, 1939–1944), 2:77.

Despite this dominant presence, however, Plato's views on education are highly contentious. Jean-Jacques Rousseau, for example, describes Plato's principal work on education, the *Republic*, as "the finest treatise on education ever written."[3] Gabriel Compayré, on the other hand, refers to it as "a compound of paradoxes and chimeras."[4] Regardless of our final assessment of Plato's educational thought, it is unquestionable that his understanding of education has had a profound impact on the development of educational theory and practice around the world for nearly two and a half millennia. The study of his views is thus of great benefit, both as a means of examining fundamental questions about the nature of education addressed in his work, and also as a means of better understanding the historical roots of the Western educational tradition. To these ends, this volume is an attempt to introduce the educational thought of Plato in a way that, while necessarily incomplete, is nevertheless thorough. The first three chapters provide a framework for understanding Plato's views on education by offering a brief biography of his life as well as describing the historical and educational contexts in which he lived and wrote. Chapters 4 and 5 then address Plato's overall understanding of what education is, the goals toward which it is directed, and his proposal for a program of education. Chapters 6 and 7 conclude the book by explaining the importance of the Platonic educational legacy and offering some suggestions regarding what Plato's views on education have to offer our own educational thought and practice in the twenty-first century.

3. Jean-Jacques Rousseau, *Émile*, trans. Barbara Foxley, The Everyman Library (London: Everyman, 1993), 8.

4. Gabriel Compayré, *The History of Pedagogy*, trans. W. H. Payne (Boston: D. C. Heath, 1899), 27.

CHAPTER ONE
A Brief Biography

The philosopher we know as Plato was born in Athens, Greece, in 427 BC and named after his grandfather Aristocles. The name "Plato" (which means "broad" in Greek) was given to him sometime during his youth, either because of his robust figure or due to the breadth of his eloquence or his forehead.[1] Although a prolific writer, he did not write much about his own life. Thus most of the personal information we have about him comes from accounts written by his contemporaries and later thinkers. His parents were Ariston and Perictione, and both came from distinguished families in the Athenian aristocracy. On his mother's side he was a descendant of the famous Athenian lawmaker Solon. His father's family included many nobles and famous Athenian statesmen as well, and both sides supposedly were descended from the god Poseidon. He had two older brothers, Adeimantus and Glaucon, as well as an older sister, Potone. When Plato was still quite young his father died, and his mother subsequently married another prominent Athenian named Pyrilampes. Through this union Plato acquired a stepsister, Demus, and later his half-brother, Antiphon, was born as well. Besides these family details, little is known about Plato's early childhood. As a young man he dreamed of devoting himself to politics, and he also had aspirations of becoming a playwright or poet. Two key events, however, led Plato to forgo these dreams and instead devote his life to philosophy—that is, to the pursuit of wisdom.[2]

---

1. Diogenes Laertius, *Lives of Eminent Philosophers*, 2 vols., trans. R. D. Hicks (Cambridge, MA: Harvard University Press, 1912), 3.4.
2. The word *philosophy* in Greek means literally "love of wisdom."

The first of these events was the Peloponnesian War between Athens and rival city-state Sparta that began in 431 BC, before Plato was born, and lasted until 404 BC. When Plato returned from fighting in the last few years of this war, he came home to a defeated Athens characterized by political, economic, moral, and social instability and dissolution. The famous Athenian democracy was abolished, and in its place thirty rulers were selected to govern Athens, in part based on their allegiance to Sparta. Known as the Tyranny of the Thirty, this group reigned from 404–403 BC, and both Plato's cousin Critias as well as his uncle Charmides were later forced out of public office because of their involvement with the Tyranny of the Thirty. Plato's aristocratic background thus became a political liability rather than an asset, and in the years after the Peloponnesian War there was no longer a comfortable place in Athenian politics for someone with his loyalties and connections.

[Plato] came home to a defeated Athens characterized by political, economic, moral, and social instability and dissolution.

The second event that changed the trajectory of Plato's life was his acquaintance with the famous philosopher Socrates. Sometime in his late teen years Plato came under the influence of Socrates, and for nearly a decade he was Socrates's friend and pupil. Although Plato became a devoted member of Socrates's intimate circle, in many ways the two men could not have been more dissimilar: Socrates was over sixty years old when he became acquainted with Plato, while Plato was younger than twenty; Socrates was the poor son of a stonemason and midwife, while Plato had a prestigious aristocratic lineage; Plato was well educated and handsome, while Socrates was a commoner known for being ugly. Despite these differences, however, Plato committed himself to learning under Socrates, and during their years together Socrates had a profound influence on Plato's life and thought.

In 399 BC Socrates was convicted by an Athenian jury of corrupting the youth of Athens and failing to revere the gods recognized by the state. He was condemned to death, and Plato was deeply disillusioned by what he viewed as the unjust execution of his mentor and friend. The passing of Socrates was arguably the event that definitively set the trajectory of Plato's life toward philosophy and not politics.[3] Soon after Socrates's death Plato withdrew from political involvement altogether and went into a self-imposed exile from Athens. During these ten years of voluntary exile, he traveled to Megara, Asia Minor, Egypt, Cyrene, Sicily, and Italy. We do not know what he did during all these years, but according to Diogenes Laertius, Plato's purpose in visiting at least some of these places was to visit with other famous philosophers.[4] While in Sicily he also spent time advising and mentoring Dionysius the Elder, who was the ruler of Syracuse.

After returning to Athens, in 387 BC, Plato founded his own school called the Academy in the grove of Academe, northwest of Athens. The Academy was situated near Colonus in a lonely and secluded sacred wood dedicated to the hero Academos. Plato chose the spot for its religious associations with nearby sanctuaries consecrated to other gods such as Poseidon, Adrastes, and Dionysus. The Academy was dedicated to the muses, patrons of literature and the arts, and during Plato's lifetime no fees were charged to students, who came to the Academy to study astronomy, biology, mathematics, political theory, and philosophy. For the rest of his life Plato lived at the Academy, though his career there was interrupted twice by trips back to Sicily, once in 367 BC and then again in 361. During these trips he continued his role as political adviser and mentor, now to Dionysius the Younger, the son and successor of Dionysius the Elder, with whom

3. See Malcolm Schofield, "Plato in His Time and Place," in *The Oxford Handbook of Plato*, ed. Gail Fine (Oxford: Oxford University Press, 2008), 41. Schofield writes that for Plato Socrates's death "crystallized the inevitability of conflict between philosophy and politics and their incommensurable assumptions."

4. Diogenes Laertius, *Lives of Eminent Philosophers* 3.6.

Plato had worked during his exile from Athens. Aside from these trips, Plato remained in Athens writing and teaching. During these years he wrote as many as thirty dialogues (twenty-five of which have been preserved) as well as a number of letters. The most famous of his works, the *Republic*, was completed around 375 BC. When Plato died in 347 BC at the age of eighty, he was buried by his friends on the grounds of the Academy.

Chapter Two
Plato's Historical Context

In order to understand Plato's views on education, it is important first to understand the historical and educational context in which he thought and wrote. The development of the Athens known by Plato began in the eighth century BC as Greek civilization started transitioning from a loose system of tribal political organization to a more formal structure of city-states. These city-states functioned as political, economic, social, and religious centers, and because they were politically independent, they were able to develop quite differently. The city-state contrasted most often with Athens is Sparta. While geographically the two cities are only ninety miles apart, by the sixth century BC they had become radically different, both politically and culturally. Sparta maintained a stable oligarchic and militaristic state, while Athens moved progressively (albeit erratically) toward democracy.

In 594 BC, the Athenian leader and first great law giver, Solon, instituted a series of reforms in response to tensions between the aristocracy and lower classes. Under his laws the lower classes were admitted into citizenship, and any citizen had the right to bring a legal charge against another citizen regardless of class differences between them. At the end of the sixth century, democracy was further institutionalized by the reforms of Cleisthenes. These reforms divided the Athenian city-state into ten distinct regions in which citizens elected leaders to serve in the various branches of government. During the fifth century, Athens continued to develop and reached its political, military, economic, and cultural height. The Persian invasions at the beginning of the century led to the formation of the Delian League—a loose association of Greek city-states that Athens quickly came to control. In large part due to its controversial role in the Delian League, Athens achieved political stability and quickly became the economic center of the Mediterranean world. High culture and the arts flourished during the middle of the century, and it was under the leadership of Pericles (circa 460–430 BC) that many of the surviving architectural achievements, such as the Parthenon, were designed and constructed. Democracy flourished during this period as well, and the years of Pericles's reign are often referred to as the "Golden Age" of Athens.

During the second half of the fifth century, the spirit of Athens continued to manifest itself in a variety of cultural forms, and there was an explosion of writing on a wide variety of topics, from horsemanship to medicine to painting techniques. Athens was known for supporting freedom and equality, and the arts, humanities, and democracy all flourished. The Athenian drama, sculpture, architecture, literature, and oratory of these years created a trajectory for centuries of Western culture, and the works of this period have been heralded as archetypes throughout history. Thus Frederick Eby and Charles Flinn Arrowood refer to the Athenians as "the best of the Greeks" and describe them as possessing "in highest measure all those qualities which have made Greece immortal. . . . They were imitative, inventive, versatile, enterprising, adventurous, extremely artistic, volatile, and always self-confident."[1] James Jarrett similarly notes that by the time of Pericles even the worst enemies of the Athenians recognized them to be "imaginative, innovative, daring, and indefatigable."[2] These characterizations of the Athenian people would not have surprised the Athenians of the fifth century, for they were self-aware and proud of their cultural

1. Frederick Eby and Charles Flinn Arrowood, *The History and Philosophy of Education Ancient and Medieval*, Prentice-Hall Education Series (New York: Prentice-Hall, 1942), 220. Cf. ibid., 287, where they write that "In no period of human history has the genius of man unfolded with greater rapidity and prodigality than in the fifth century B.C."

2. James Jarrett, *The Educational Theories of the Sophists*, Classics in Education 39 (New York: Teachers College Press, 1969), 2.

achievements. In his 429 BC funeral oration, for example, Pericles says of his fellow Athenians that:

> We are lovers of the beautiful, yet simple in our tastes, and we cultivate the mind without loss of manliness. . . . To sum up: I say that Athens is the school of Hellas [Greece], and that the individual Athenian in his own person seems to have the power of adapting himself to the most varied forms of action with the utmost versatility and grace. This is no passing and idle word, but truth and fact; and the assertion is verified by the position to which these qualities have raised the state.[3]

Despite the remarkable achievements of fifth-century Athens, there was a dark side to the culture of this period as well. While Athenians demonstrated remarkable ingenuity, innovation, and initiative, these qualities sometimes were not well controlled. Consider, for example, the description of the Athenian people offered by a Corinthian envoy to Sparta during the Peloponnesian War: "They are revolutionary, equally quick in the conception and in the execution of every new plan. . . . They are bold beyond their strength; they run risks which prudence would condemn. . . . If a man should say of them, in a word, that they were born neither to have peace themselves, nor to allow peace to other men, he would simply speak the truth."[4] During these glory years of Athens, moral debauchery was rampant, and, intoxicated with their many successes, Athenians were known for being arrogant, superficial, and notoriously litigious.[5] Furthermore, while democracy flourished for the citizens of Athens,

---

3. Thucydides, *The History of Thucydides*, 3 vols., trans. Benjamin Jowett (New York: The Tandy-Thomas Company, 1909), 2.40–41.
4. Ibid., 1.70.
5. See Eby and Arrowood, *History and Philosophy of Education*, 223: "The Athenians were vain, shallow, and temperamental, and incapable of a deep sense of obligation to any supreme moral law. They were deficient in reverence and loyalty and were given on all occasions to accusing each other in the courts of violations of law. Finally, they were rhetorical, dramatic, talkative, wrangling, outstanding representatives of the sunny pagan spirit."

these citizens were significantly outnumbered by the slaves on whose backs many of their cultural achievements were built.[6]

Despite the remarkable achievements of fifth-century Athens, there was a dark side to the culture of this period as well.

The rapid development of Athens throughout its golden age experienced a significant setback at the end of Pericles's reign, when Athens was invaded by Sparta and thus entered into the Peloponnesian War. The war lasted for most of the rest of the fifth century, and when Athens finally was defeated, it was left broken and bitter. Having lost much of its wealth, military power, and confidence, a disillusioned Athens was now faced with the question of how to move forward and make sense of its fall from dominance. Even before the Peloponnesian War, however, the ethos of Athenian culture had begun undergoing significant shifts. Throughout the fifth century Athens's many successes were accompanied by a new set of values that undermined longstanding mores and beliefs. There was a widespread loss of reverence for the gods and national heroes, and traditional authorities such as parents and elders were not as highly respected as they previously had been. Social unity was threatened by the growth of individualism, and faith in traditionally held certainties and the moral authority of those beliefs was in decline.

Plato thus was born into a period of Athenian history characterized by great turbulence and transition. Fifth-century Athens embodied an unparalleled concentration of cultural achievement,

6. Estimates vary widely on how many citizens and slaves were living in Athens during the fifth century. During the age of Pericles there were probably somewhere between 25,000 and 50,000 citizens and somewhere between 200,000 and 400,000 slaves. In addition to these two main social groups, there also were a smaller number of foreign residents known as "metics." These metics were not full citizens, though they did receive protection from the law and share in some of the full citizens' civic responsibilities.

and its rapid development and decline during those years created more questions than answers. It was the decline of Athens and the presence of these questions, however, that formed a context for Plato's philosophical thought.[7] Although he stands as the high point of Greek philosophy, in terms of Athens's political and cultural prominence Plato lived in the shadow of its zenith. Less than a decade after his death Athens was conquered by Philip of Macedon, and never again would Athens experience the glory of its fifth-century golden age. Through Philip's son Alexander the Great, however, the culture and values that developed in Athens during the fifth century were carried far beyond Athens's borders. It is largely because of this Hellenization that the remarkable Athenian achievements of the fifth century were spread around the world and became the foundation of Western culture.

Although he stands as the high point of Greek philosophy, in terms of Athens's political and cultural prominence Plato lived in the shadow of its zenith.

7. See Robert Ulich, *History of Educational Thought* (New York: American Book Company, 1945), 3: In Plato's day "Greece was shattered to pieces and in utter need of moral and educational regeneration. The Athenian *polis* had been defeated by the Spartans. Common faith and customs had crumbled; teachers and philosophers were necessary in order to give the people, through reasoning, what earlier generations had achieved through tradition, voluntary loyalty, and communal responsibility."

Chapter Three
Plato's Educational Context

In addition to the political and cultural changes happening in Athens during Plato's day, there also were significant educational transitions taking place. In order to set the context for Plato's educational thought, it is first of all necessary again to contrast Athens with its fellow city-state Sparta. Sparta was, above all else, a military state. As such, its system of education was designed to produce warriors equipped to serve the interests of the state. The control and defense of Spartan territory was the primary goal of its citizens' education, while the development of those citizens as distinct individuals was overlooked almost entirely. In other words, the purpose of the education system was explicitly the survival of the state, not the flourishing of individuals. Almost from birth a child's education was controlled by the state. Every baby boy was presented to a committee of elders, and the committee made a decision as to whether or not the baby had the potential to become a strong warrior-citizen. If the child passed the examination, he was returned to his parents for care until he reached the age of seven. If the committee deemed the baby not to be fine-looking, healthy, and well-formed, however, he was taken to a place near Mount Taygetus and simply left exposed to die.[1] While infant exposure was a fairly common practice throughout the ancient world, the Spartan distinctive was that the state determined which children were deemed fit to live and which were killed.

Formal education for boys who survived childhood began at age seven, and for eleven years they lived away from home in mili-

1. Plutarch, *Lycurgus* 16. All Plutarch citations are from *A Selection of Nine Greek Lives*, trans. Robin Waterfield, Oxford World's Classics (Oxford: Oxford University Press, 1998).

tary-style barracks under severe conditions. Given that "the supreme purpose of the development of the Spartan male was to become a brave and ruthless warrior, . . . the content and method of education from beginning to end was determined by militaristic considerations."[2] The children went barefoot in winter and summer alike, wore only a single garment, and were systematically underfed. Theft was encouraged, and if apprehended students were punished for their clumsiness in being caught, not for their thieving itself. Having developed the physical training and morale necessary to serve as soldiers, at age eighteen they began intensive military training that usually was followed by ten years of military service. Not until age thirty did they become full-fledged citizens, and for another thirty years until age sixty they remained on active military reserve.

The education of Spartan girls, unlike that of the boys, took place in their homes instead of at the barracks. Like their male counterparts, however, Spartan females were trained for service to the state. They were taught the requisite skills for running a household, including instruction on how to manage slaves. They also were required to engage in physical training so as to prepare their bodies for bearing and rearing strong sons for the military. Thus from beginning to end both boys and girls were trained under the auspices of the state for the purposes of the state. As Drever succinctly explains, "The most striking characteristic of the Spartan educational system is the fact that it was a system under State control, education being conducted entirely by the State, at the expense of the State, and for the ends of the State."[3]

As in Sparta, education in Athens was for centuries driven almost exclusively by the needs of the military. By the fifth century, however, there was a clear distinction between Spartan education, in which this

2. Ralph L. Pounds, *The Development of Education in Western Culture* (New York: Appleton-Century-Crofts, 1968), 45.

3. James Drever, *Greek Education: Its Practice and Principles* (Cambridge: Cambridge University Press, 1912), 11.

tradition continued, and education in Athens, in which intellectual interests had become much more prominent. Whereas in Sparta the prosperity of the state was pursued by turning individual citizens into indistinguishable cogs in the state's militaristic machine, Athenian education came to embrace the view that "the full and free development of the individual, in the harmonious exercise of all his powers, was the best way to secure the happiness and prosperity of the State."[4] In other words, the purpose of Athenian education was to develop students *as holistic individuals*, not merely as generic warriors whose individual development was dictated and limited by their military function. As Frederick Eby and Charles Flinn Arrowood explain:

> Athenian education sought to mold the boy into an integrated whole through a cultivation of all aspects of his nature. To be a perfect man involved the exercise of all human functions, family life, politics, war, and physical, moral, intellectual, and aesthetic activity. Body and soul, the real and the ideal, individual and public interests, the beautiful and the good, the intellectual and the aesthetic, the rough virtue of the fighter and the urbane qualities of the gentleman, were all to be skillfully blended into a single personality.[5]

Unlike in Sparta where the state controlled almost every aspect of a child's formal education, in Athens the locus of responsibility lay with parents. Primarily a privilege of the aristocratic class, formal education usually consisted of parents contracting with a private tutor to provide instruction for their children. Sometime during the

---

4. Ibid., 22.
5. Frederick Eby and Charles Flinn Arrowood, *The History and Philosophy of Education Ancient and Medieval*, Prentice-Hall Education Series (New York: Prentice-Hall, 1942), 232. Cf. ibid., 225: "In Sparta, the individual was absolutely sacrificed to the state, and his training was entirely under public auspices. The Spartans developed to the utmost extreme the original capacity of the Hellenic nature for discipline and regimentation. The Athenians, on the other hand, shared the same native talent but chose to develop to the other extreme the capacity for rich and varied expression. Athens was the first state in the world's history where all human capacities were allowed to develop freely."

seventh century BC, formal schools started to appear in Athens where children could be sent to receive an education. As Athens moved from aristocracy toward democracy throughout the fifth century, education increasingly became available for all free citizens. This heightened demand for education in turn led to the creation and development of more schools. While some families continued to employ individual tutors, that method of educating the young largely gave way to the new institutions of centralized education. Unlike schools in Sparta, however, Athenian schools were not compulsory nor were they administered by the state (except schools for orphans). Rather the schools were privately operated and attended voluntarily, according to the decisions of parents. The Athenian state did take, nonetheless, great interest in the education of its citizens. From the educational reforms of Solon in the early sixth century onward, numerous laws were passed pertaining to educational matters.

> *The purpose of Athenian education was to develop students* **as holistic individuals,** *not merely as generic warriors whose individual development was dictated and limited by their military function.*

Formal education for Athenian boys usually began about age seven. The child transitioned from being under the care of a nurse and attendant to being under the charge of a pedagogue who accompanied the child through all aspects of his training: He awoke the boy in the morning, helped him get ready, escorted him to his classes at school, carried his materials, compelled him to study, helped him to review his lessons, etc. For close to a decade the student lived and worked under the all- encompassing supervision of his pedagogue, though his actual academic instruction came from various teachers and/or tutors. After these years the student's formal education ended, though sometime during the fifth century Athens began requiring that young men complete two years of military training as cadets, from ages eighteen to twenty, and then pass an examination in order to graduate as full Athenian citizens. Unlike in Sparta, there was no system of formal education for Athenian girls. In Athens education was almost exclusively for men, while women for the most part stayed at home and had limited participation in society outside their domestic realm.

The curriculum studied by Athenian boys was guided by the belief that education should train all aspects of a child's nature. Whereas in Sparta physical strength and skill were the primary goals, in Athens the curriculum was designed to develop both the body and the mind. This dual focus was recognized at least as far back as Solon, who placed physical and intellectual training on the same footing and argued that above all else children should learn "to swim and read."[6] Thus the Athenian curriculum consisted of both gymnastics for the cultivation of the body and music for the cultivation of the mind and soul. Plato, as we will see, is in many ways a proponent of this approach to education. He begins his treatment of education in the *Republic*, for example, by asking, "What will their education be? Or is it hard to find anything better than that which has developed over a long period—physical training for bodies and music and poetry for the soul?"[7] Gymnastic training included wrestling, running, jumping, training in warfare, and other exercises. Musical training included singing and playing an instrument (often the lyre). It also, however, included all the arts fostered by the muses to promote beauty and happiness. The term *music* therefore referred to a broad swath of subjects, including melody, rhythm, poetry, memorization, history, mythology, science, philosophy, and moral/aesthetic cultivation. Reading, writing, and arithmetic, sometimes collectively referred to as

---

6. See Gabriel Compayré, *The History of Pedagogy*, trans. W. H. Payne (Boston: D. C. Heath, 1899), 19. Cf. James Jarrett, *The Educational Theories of the Sophists*, Classics in Education 39 (New York: Teachers College Press, 1969), 18: "Schooling in the fifth century B.C. was, as we might say, humanistic, as well as heavily athletic."
7. Plato, *Republic* 376e2–4. All Plato citations are from Plato's *Complete Works* edited by John M. Cooper (Indianapolis: Hackett, 1997).

the grammar curriculum, also were included under the broad heading of musical training. Thus, as Eby and Arrowood point out, "In this comprehensive sense, music was the central feature of the Athenian curriculum."[8] This "musical" education was based, above all else, on the study and memorization of past poets, particularly Homer. Plato refers to Homer as "the poet who educated Greece,"[9] and for centuries Greek education relied upon Homer as its primary text. Students learned to sing or chant the works of Homer and other lyric poets, and public contests regularly were held at which prizes were given for the best recitations.

The curriculum studied by Athenian boys was guided by the belief that education should train all aspects of a child's nature.

The goal of this educational system, unlike that of Spartan education, was to produce men of both sound mind and sound body. Certainly Athenians wanted to educate the young for citizenship and service to the state. Unlike the Spartans, however, they believed that good citizens were those who were not merely trained as warriors but rather those who demonstrated *arête* ("virtue" or "excellence") in all areas of life.[10] They viewed beauty and goodness as a unified whole, and the guiding ideal of this *paideia*, or "education," was expressed by the Greek word *kalokagathia*, which means "being both beautiful and good."[11] Technical vocational training simply had no place

---

8. Eby and Arrowood, *History and Philosophy of Education*, 254. Cf. Compayré, *History of Pedagogy*, 20. "Music held a large place in the actual life of the Greeks. The laws were promulgated in song. It was necessary to sing in order to fulfill one's religious duties. It was held that the education of Themistocles had been neglected because he had not learned music."

9. Plato, *Republic* 606e2.

10. *Arête* is an interesting word that is not exactly translatable into English. Most often it is translated as "virtue" or "excellence." At times the term is used to refer to specific virtues (courage, justice, temperance, piety, moderation, wisdom, etc.). It also can be used, however, in a more general sense as a broad category that includes multiple individual virtues.

11. The word is a combination of *kalos* ("beautiful") and *agathos* ("good").

in their paradigm of education. Given the prevalence of slaves in fifth-century Athens, the vast majority of educated citizens did not engage in manual labor or have any need to learn a technical trade. Instead they were at leisure to devote themselves to the "higher" study of art, science, philosophy, politics, and education. Leisure, as they understood it, was not the absence of work but rather "work done for the love of it."[12] In other words, education was not merely a necessary step for the achieving of some extrinsic goal such as the acquisition of a particular job; rather, education was understood as an activity of leisure in that students could devote themselves freely to it as an end in and of itself. Leisure and education thus were closely entwined notions, and it is from *skole*, the Greek word for "leisure," that the English word *school* is derived.[13]

This understanding and method of education, known as the "old education" in Athens, flourished during the first half of the fifth century. In contrast to this "old education," however, during the second half of the century Athens underwent a transition as changing social and political realities gave rise to a "new education." By the time of Pericles, Athens was the economic, political, and commercial center of Greece. This made a successful career in Athenian politics increasingly prestigious and lucrative.[14] The political landscape was changing, however, and becoming more and more democratic. In this new political climate, successful politicians were those who had mastered the art of public speaking and could use the tools of rhetoric to argue persuasively. As Rachana Kamtekar explains:

---

12. Bernard Bosanquet, *The Education of the Young in the "Republic" of Plato* (Cambridge: Cambridge University Press, 1917), 12.

13. For an extended treatment of the concept of leisure and its relationship to education, see Josef Pieper's classic book *Leisure, the Basis of Culture*, trans. Alexander Dru (Indianapolis: Liberty Fund, 1999).

14. See H. I. Marrou, *A History of Education in Antiquity*, trans. George Lamb, Wisconsin Studies in Classics (Madison: University of Wisconsin Press, 1982), 47. Marrou describes how in Athens there developed "an intensely active political life; and exercise of power, the management of affairs, became the essential concern, the noblest, the most highly-prized activity in the eyes of every Greek, the ultimate aim of his ambition."

> Athenian political life had changed radically through the fifth century, with reforms in democratic institutions making possible greater popular participation (for example, jury duty and assembly attendance were now compensated for by a day's wage), at the same time as Athens's imperial pursuits greatly complicated its political affairs. Would-be political leaders now had to communicate effectively with a wider cast of people than previously and on a wider range of affairs. Now successful political leadership called for expertise in public speaking; expertise in military strategy, once a prerequisite for leadership, became dispensable.[15]

Thus there was in the middle of the fifth century a tension between the conservative old education's emphasis on physical skills and respect for the Greek literary tradition, and the new education's focus on verbal skills and respect for eloquent and persuasive speech. Learning to speak eloquently and persuasively, however, required a kind of training that previously had been absent from Athenian education. The old education thus was exposed as ill equipped to prepare students for civic success. A new kind of education was needed that taught citizens not primarily how to be good and beautiful, but rather how to master the *techne* of eloquent and persuasive speech.

It was within this context that a group of teachers known as Sophists came on the scene, claiming to provide a new type of education that could meet the new demands of the times. Sophist thinkers such as Protagoras, Prodicus, Hippias, and Gorgias rejected traditional moral standards and maintained that there

---

15. Rachana Kamtekar, "Plato on Education and Art," in *The Oxford Handbook of Plato*, ed. Gail Fine (Oxford: Oxford University Press, 2008), 337. Cf. Jarrett, *Educational Theories of the Sophists*, 3: "In the middle of the fifth century B.C. there was a verbal explosion of unprecedented magnitude. . . . It is as if, at a signal, everybody began talking at once. Men argued, debated, soliloquized, declaimed, contradicted, orated. In trade, in politics, in litigation, in estate management, in war, in courtship, in international relations, he who had the gift of words was victor."

are no universal or absolute standards by which truth or goodness can be evaluated. "Man is the measure of all things," Protagoras famously declared,[16] and thus what is true for the individual man is true; what is good for the individual man is good. The Sophists argued that laws and moral codes are merely of human origin and that as such they are imperfect and unreliable guides to human behavior. Given that there are no absolute values or standards, either for individuals or for governments, everything is a matter of expediency. The successful person is therefore one who is able to turn circumstances to his own advantage.[17] The ability to sway public opinion was essential for political success in Athens, and the Sophists recognized that "in political life absolute theoretical truth is irrelevant; it is success that counts."[18]

The Sophists' approach to education therefore was thoroughly and unabashedly pragmatic and utilitarian. Their goal was to teach students the art of politics, and in order to do so they had to teach them the arts of persuasion. The Sophists were not concerned with teaching knowledge of the truth but with teaching the ability to win arguments and convince an audience of any proposition whatsoever. Thus their curriculum focused on the skills of dialectic and rhetoric: how to ask and answer questions, pit one theory against another, and speak eloquently and persuasively. In sharp contrast to the goals of the "old education," these skills were entirely instrumental in that they were not ends in and of themselves. Dissociated completely from truth or virtue, it was up to students whether to use the skills they had been taught for good or ill.[19] Education for the Sophists, therefore, was not a matter of nurturing human beings in any

16. See Plato, *Theaetetus* 152a23.
17. Frank M. Flanagan, *The Greatest Educators Ever* (London: Continuum, 2006), 5–6.
18. Samuel Scolnicov, *Plato's Metaphysics of Education* (London: Routledge, 1988), 4–5. Cf. Flanagan, *Greatest Educators Ever*, 6: "It is not too fanciful to assert that the Sophists' role in ancient Greece was similar to that of image consultants who currently provide media training for politicians and others."
19. See Flanagan, *Greatest Educators Ever*, 6: "What the Sophists promised was a strictly utilitarian technical education unaffected by issues of morality or human goodness."

holistic sense. Rather it was simply a matter of offering students the technical skills they needed to be politically successful in the current social context. Instead of opening schools, the Sophists gathered groups of students around them in a form of collective tutoring. They took charge of their students' education in its entirety, usually for a period of three to four years. Starting with Protagoras, they charged money for their services, and many were paid handsomely enough to become quite wealthy.

Not surprisingly, despite their financial success the Sophists faced harsh criticism from those who did not accept their relativistic and pragmatic approach to education. Almost all of the Sophists' writings are lost to us, and thus our knowledge of them comes primarily from secondhand sources. Plato, the principle source of this knowledge, was clearly biased against them.[20] On his view the Sophists were not true philosophers (lovers of wisdom) but deceptive rhetoricians. He draws a hard distinction between the Sophists, those who through themselves to be wise and capable of making others wise, and true philosophers, who ardently searched for wisdom but also humbly recognized their own ignorance.[21] Plato also is critical of the Sophists for accepting money for their teaching.[22] Despite these negative assessments, the Sophists undeniably made a number of novel and important contributions to the history of Athenian education. For one thing, they were the first professional educators, and some credit them with

---

20. Another criticism of the Sophists can be found in Aristophanes's comedy *The Clouds*. This play pokes fun at thinkers who are interested only in winning arguments and not in promoting truth and virtue, though ironically the chief culprit in the play is Socrates. Although in Plato's *Symposium* Aristophanes appears to be on friendly terms with Socrates, his play almost certainly influenced the public's opinion of Socrates as a Sophist who was corrupting the youth of Athens.

21. See Pieper, *Leisure, the Basis of Culture*, 111: "The words philosopher and philosophy were coined, according to legend—and the legend is of great antiquity—by Pythagoras in explicit contrast to the words *sophia* and *sophos*: no man is wise, and no man 'knows'; God alone is wise and all-knowing. At the very most a man might call himself a lover of wisdom and a seeker after knowledge—a philosopher." It is interesting that despite the actual meaning of the word *sophist* (literally, "wise one") throughout history the negative judgment of the Sophists has prevailed such that words like "sophist," "sophistry," and "sophistical" generally have had negative connotations.

22. See, for example, Plato, *Apology* 19d4–20c3.

inventing both the theory and the philosophy of education.[23] They also introduced grammar as a distinct aspect of the curriculum and were largely responsible for the development of dialectic as a curricular subject as well. Furthermore, before the Sophists, political success was primarily a function of the family into which one was born, not a matter of formal training. The Sophists' approach, however, made political success dependent on merit and education, not merely on one's family connections. Thus despite their faults, the Sophists "may be said to have established, once and for all, the necessity of higher education conducted by professionals."[24] Perhaps more significant than any of these contributions, however, the Sophists were largely responsible for creating the background of educational thought and practice against which Plato developed his own views on education. Having outlined the historical and educational context of Plato's work, it is to his understanding of education that we now turn.

---

23. See, for example, Werner Jaeger, *Paideia: The Ideals of Greek Culture*, trans. Gilbert Highet (New York: Oxford University Press, 1939–1944), 1:293.

24. Jarrett, *Educational Theories of the Sophists*, 108.

CHAPTER FOUR
Plato's Understanding of the Nature and Purpose of Education

Plato's views on education, compared to the landscape of Athenian education during his lifetime, are squarely conservative. In sharp contrast to the Sophists, he is not a relativist but maintains that absolute truth exists as well as universal moral standards. Throughout his writings Plato continually seeks to refute various forms of relativism, and his philosophical inquiries are predicated unequivocally on the assumption that there are in fact universal truths about the nature of reality.[1] H. I. Marrou therefore writes that, in opposition to the Sophists' concern with immediate practical results, "Plato built his system of education on a fundamental belief in truth, and on the conquest of truth by rational knowledge. . . . Plato's criterion was not success but truth."[2] Above all else, the truth for which Plato searches is truth about the nature of virtue. Throughout his dialogues Socrates continually converses with his interlocutors in order to discover the nature of various virtues (piety in the *Euthyphro*, justice in the *Republic*, courage in the *Laches*, the

1. This assumption follows from his theory of the Forms, or Ideas, which is a central underlying tenet of his thought. (The Greek *eidos* which in this context is usually translated as "form" also can mean "outward appearance," "kind," or "sight.") According to Plato everything in our world (the world of appearances) is a reflection or imitation of archetypal Forms that exist in a different world, the world of reality. These Forms exist as real entities, but not in our world of space and time. Rather they are unchanging categories that serve as the patterns that objects in our world imitate or participate in. As transcendent universal and eternal standards, they are the basis on which we describe and categorize things in our world in various ways. For example, an object is beautiful insofar as it imitates the Form of Beauty; an action is just insofar as it partakes in the Form of Justice; a statement is true insofar as it participates in the Form of Truth; etc. According to Plato the highest form of knowledge is to be acquainted with the Forms as objects of thought.
2. H. I. Marrou, *A History of Education in Antiquity*, trans. George Lamb, Wisconsin Studies in Classics (Madison: University of Wisconsin Press, 1982), 66.

nature of virtue itself in the *Meno*, etc.). The virtues play such a central role in Plato's thought that some have argued the search for the nature of virtue is the starting point for all of his philosophy. Werner Jaeger goes even further, contending that "Plato's Socrates is *exclusively* concerned with the problem of virtue."[3] Again, underlying Plato's search for the nature of virtue is the unequivocal assumption that the virtues are universal moral goods. The notion that moral goodness is reducible to personal expediency is thoroughly rejected, both implicitly and explicitly. Present all throughout his work, this is seen perhaps most explicitly in book 1 of the *Republic* where Socrates argues against Thrasymachus's definition of justice as "nothing other than the advantage of the stronger."[4]

Above all else, the truth for which Plato searches is truth about the nature of virtue.

Like all great educational thinkers throughout history, Plato understands education to be fundamentally teleological. That is to say, any style of education has, whether explicitly or implicitly, a goal or goals toward which it is directed.[5] Again, a conservative relative to the Athens of his day, Plato echoes the old education and maintains that the purpose of education is to develop men who exhibit *kalokagathia*, i.e., whose lives embody the beautiful and the good. In the *Republic*, for example, he writes that, "The final outcome of education, I suppose we'd say, is a single newly finished person, who is either good or the opposite."[6] He goes on to argue that, "The form of the good is the most important thing to learn about" and that, "It's by their relation

3. Werner Jaeger, *Paideia: The Ideals of Greek Culture*, trans. Gilbert Highet (New York: Oxford University Press, 1939–1944), 2:91 (emphasis mine).

4. Plato, *Republic* 338c1–2.

5. See Jaeger, *Paideia*, 2:154, where Jaeger argues that according to Plato, "The problem at the root of all education is to find, to define, and to understand the standard by which it is to be regulated. [The *Gorgias*, for example,] presents Socrates as the only true teacher, because he alone knows the *telos*." Cf. Richard Livingstone, *Plato and Modern Education*, The Rede Lecture 1944 (Cambridge: Cambridge University Press, 1944), 30: "The first step to good education is a clear view of what human beings should be."

6. Plato, *Republic* 425c3–4.

to it that just things and the others become useful and beneficial."[7] In the *Laws* he similarly claims that what he means by "education" is not training for a particular trade or business but "education from childhood in *virtue*."[8] He explains that this virtue consists in having one's loves properly aligned such that one adores what is good and abhors what is not: "There is one element you could isolate in any account you give, and this is the correct formation of our feelings of pleasure and pain, which makes us hate what we ought to hate from first to last, and love what we ought to love. Call this 'education,' and I, at any rate, think you would be giving it its proper name."[9] Thus, as Jaeger correctly notes, coming to apprehend the good is "the intention of *all* education in Plato."[10]

Two important points about this understanding of education should be highlighted. The first is that it has very little to do with the teaching of practical technical skills. That is to say, Plato's understanding of education is wholly liberal as opposed to a conception of education in which its primary purpose is training for some technical vocation. In the *Laws*, for example, he writes that "A training directed to acquiring money or a robust physique, or even to some intellectual facility not guided by reason and justice, we should want to call coarse and illiberal, and say that it had no claim whatever to be called education."[11] The primary purpose of education is thus not to transfer to students a body of knowledge or a set of skills. Rather it is to cultivate them into a certain type

7. Ibid., 505a1–3. Plato goes on to defend this claim and concludes that, "What gives truth to the things known and the power to know to the knower is the form of the good. And though it is the cause of knowledge and truth, it is also an object of knowledge. Both knowledge and truth are beautiful things, but the good is other and more beautiful than they" (*Republic* 508d9–e4). Cf. ibid., 517b7–c3: "In the knowable realm, the form of the good is the last thing to be seen, and it is reached only with difficulty. Once one has seen it, however, one must conclude that it is the cause of all that is correct and beautiful in anything. . . . In the intelligible realm it controls and provides truth and understanding."

8. Plato, *Laws* 643e4 (emphasis original).

9. Ibid., 653b6–c4.

10. Jaeger, *Paideia*, 2:315 (emphasis original).

11. Plato, *Laws* 644a3–6.

of human beings who have a certain disposition toward learning, themselves, and the world around them. In contrast to the Sophists, whose primary goal was to equip their students with practical skills that would enable them to be successful in Athenian society, for Plato the aim of education is "ultimately right conduct, not success in life."[12]

The second related point to emphasize about Plato's view of education is that it is concerned principally with moral formation and not merely with the acquisition of knowledge.[13] As Richard Livingstone correctly points out, "For Plato the supreme aim of education is human goodness. . . . So he conceives education essentially as a training in values. This seems to me the most important truth that we can learn from Plato."[14] Thus the most significant educational question according to Plato is not what a person knows but how a person lives. Education is most fundamentally concerned with conduct, not with knowledge. The problem with knowledge, argues Plato, is that it can be used for good or for ill. In the *Republic*, for example, Socrates explains that "The one who is most able to guard against disease is also most able to produce it unnoticed" and that the person who is clever at guarding money "must also be clever at stealing it."[15] Knowledge, in other words, is not an intrinsic good,

---

12. James Drever, *Greek Education: Its Practice and Principles* (Cambridge: Cambridge University Press, 1912), 57–58.

13. It is important to note that while terms such as *good* (*kalos*) and *virtue* (*arête*) do have moral overtones for Plato, they are not exclusively moral terms. Rather they refer to the capability or power of a thing to fulfill its purpose or nature. Thus a knife is "good" insofar as it is able cut well, i.e., to fulfill its purpose as a knife. A cow is "excellent" insofar as it is capable of producing milk—i.e., of fulfilling its purpose as a cow. Similarly, the "goodness" or "virtue" of a person is the quality that enables a person to fulfill his purpose and live according to his true nature.

14. Livingstone, *Plato and Modern Education*, 12. Cf. Frederick Eby and Charles Flinn Arrowood, *The History and Philosophy of Education Ancient and Medieval*, Prentice-Hall Education Series (New York: Prentice-Hall, 1942), 362–363: "Plato accepted the common understanding of all antiquity that education is a process of moral training. It is the voluntary effort of the older generation to pass on to the younger the good habits of living and the wisdom gathered from experience." Eby and Arrowood go on to say that "The fundamental process of early education is the inculcation of moral attitudes and habits" (ibid., 372).

15. Plato, *Republic* 333e6–7, 334a5–6.

for without a moral compass to guide its use it can bring about great evil. As Jim Garrison trenchantly points out, "Even if someone had complete knowledge of the world as it actually is, even if that person could complete the mistaken quest for absolute certainty, the moral questions would remain: What should I do?"[16] In the *Euthydemus* Plato makes a similar point about supposed goods such as wealth, health, and good looks. Unless the use of these things is guided by wisdom, he argues, "They are greater evils than their opposites."[17] The purpose of education is therefore intrinsically moral in nature, and the ultimate goal is to form students who are equipped with wisdom, with an understanding of the good, such that they can use whatever knowledge they may possess in ways that are virtuous.[18]

The most significant educational question according to Plato is not what a person knows but how a person lives. Education is most fundamentally concerned with conduct, not with knowledge.

This understanding of the goal of education significantly affects how Plato understands the value and purpose of various curricular subjects. In fact, he is explicit that the subjects he thinks should be studied are selected not on the basis of their content per se but rather because of their ability to turn the soul away from darkness and toward goodness and truth.[19] He admonishes that, "Each of us must neglect all other subjects and be most concerned to seek out and learn those that will enable him to distinguish the good life from the

16. Jim Garrison, *Dewey and Eros: Wisdom and Desire in the Art of Teaching*, Advances in Contemporary Educational Thought Series 19 (New York: Teachers College Press, 1997), 1.
17. Plato, *Euthydemus* 281d7. Cf. ibid., *Meno* 87e1–89a2.
18. See Jaeger, *Paideia*, 2:69: "Education is not the cultivation of certain abilities; it is not the communication of certain branches of knowledge—at least all that is significant only as a means and a stage in the process of education."
19. See Plato, *Republic* 521c4–d1.

bad and always to make the best choice possible in every situation."[20] Plato thus clearly recognizes that the curricular subjects are not ends in and of themselves but are educationally valuable only insofar as they promote the realization of education's ultimate goals.

The study of gymnastics, for example, is not merely physical training for the development of certain skills. Rather its purpose is to cultivate a whole and balanced person whose body and mind function together in harmony. Thus Plato contends that the person of understanding "will always cultivate the harmony of his body for the sake of the consonance in his soul."[21] Plato warns of the imbalance that will occur if physical training was neglected or overemphasized and argues that an appropriate focus on physical training will foster a soul that is balanced between the extremes of savagery and overcultivation.[22] Thus as Gabriel Compayré succinctly notes, physical training in Plato's thought receives "great emphasis, not as an end in itself, but as a means towards mental and spiritual health."[23]

The study of music similarly is intended not merely to equip students with a set of skills. Rather the point is that by studying beautiful works of art and music students are directed toward morality, for it is through the beautiful that the soul rises toward the good. By memorizing the works of great poets, students are exposed to exemplars of human greatness and learn to appreciate and imitate them. By studying the nature of rhythm and harmony, students' souls themselves become harmoniously ordered. By developing a sense of taste, students are equipped to be pleased by fine things and therefore allow those things into their souls to nurture them in goodness.[24] That

20. Ibid., 618b8–c3.

21. Ibid., 591c8–d1. Cf. Robert Ulich, *History of Educational Thought* (New York: American Book Company, 1945), 4. "Plato starts by emphasizing the necessity of sound interaction between body and mind as the basis of all education."

22. Plato, *Republic* 410c7–e2.

23. Gabriel Compayré, *The History of Pedagogy*, trans. W. H. Payne (Boston: D. C. Heath, 1899), 41.

24. See Plato, *Republic* 401d4–402a4.

Plato views musical education as an inherently moral enterprise can be seen clearly in the careful attention he gives to which stories, songs, and poems should be taught to young children. He is adamant that children not be exposed to stories that are false or give a bad image of the gods and heroes. Rather stories should be selected "whenever they are fine or beautiful and [rejected] when they aren't,"[25] with the goal of developing students who are "as god-fearing and godlike as human beings can be."[26] Thus while Plato does advocate for a robust censorship of the arts, his goal is not to ideologically brainwash students or to restrict their exposure to ideas with which he happens to disagree. Rather his view is based on the way in which he understands moral formation to take place in young children. He recognizes that the beliefs children form at a young age "are hard to erase and apt to become unalterable,"[27] and he wants to ensure that as children formulate their basic understanding of the world their conceptions are accurate and will not inhibit their moral development.

In addition to gymnastics and music, Plato also explicitly addresses the purpose of studying the four sciences that together comprise the traditional Pythagorean quadrivium: arithmetic, geometry, astronomy, and harmonics (music in our more narrow contemporary use of the term). With regard to arithmetic Plato writes that it is educationally valuable not because it enables us to carry out business but because it leads us toward truth and the ability to grasp being. He therefore argues that the true purpose of education in arithmetic is not "like tradesmen and retailers, for the sake of buying and selling, but . . . for ease in turning the soul around, away from becoming and towards

---

25. Ibid., 377b8–c1.

26. Ibid., 383c2–3. Throughout books II and III of the *Republic* Plato spends a great deal of time elaborating on how stories, songs, and poems should be selected. See ibid., 424b5–7, where he says that in order to avoid the corruption of education, rulers must "above all [guard] as carefully as they can against any innovation in music and poetry or in physical training that is counter to the established order." He goes on to say that he is convinced that changes in musical forms always bring about changes in the city's laws (ibid., 424c4–5).

27. Ibid., 378d6–7.

truth and being."[28] He likewise defines geometry as "knowledge of what always is"[29] and argues that it "draws the soul towards truth and produces philosophical thought by directing upwards what we now wrongly direct downwards."[30] Astronomy is praised because it "compels the soul to look upward and leads it from things here to things there,"[31] and he claims that the study of harmonics is "useful in the search for the beautiful and the good. But pursued for any other purpose, it's useless."[32] The study of these subjects is thus highly valuable, but not because of any immediate practical ends. Plato certainly recognizes that the study of these disciplines does have ancillary practical value.[33] His essential point, however, is that these practical benefits are not the primary reason why the disciplines should be studied. Their purpose is not "simply to provide technical training: however practical they might be, they nevertheless [have] a much deeper function."[34]

While Plato writes at great length about the purpose of education as the cultivation of harmoniously balanced individuals, he also is clear that this is not education's ultimate end. The ultimate goal is not a well-ordered individual but a well-ordered state. Consider, for example, his definition of education as "a training which produces a keen desire to become a perfect citizen who knows how to rule and be ruled as justice demands."[35] While the goodness of the individual certainly is an intermediate goal, it is a goodness that directs the individual beyond

28. Ibid., 525c2–4. Cf. ibid., 522e4, where he says that the study of arithmetic is necessary in order "to be properly human."

29. Ibid., 527b7.

30. Ibid., 527b8–9.

31. Ibid., 529a1–2.

32. Ibid., 531c6–7.

33. See, for example, ibid., 522e3–4; 526d1–5.

34. Marrou, *History of Education in Antiquity*, 73. Cf. Richard Nettleship, *The Theory of Education in the "Republic" of Plato*, Classics in Education 36 (New York: Teachers College Press, 1968), 119–120: "Plato's conception, then, of the educational function of the sciences is, primarily, that they may be used to teach men to think. . . . The study has to him a real as well as a formal significance. It serves not only as a mental gymnastic, helping the soul to reach the place where the truth is to be found, but also as an actual introduction to the truth for which it is looking."

35. Plato, *Laws* 643e4–6.

his own development and toward the development of the state. Plato maintains, in other words, that "Individual development is by no means an end in itself, or an absolute 'good,' but only an end in relation to the higher end, the prosperity and wellbeing of the State."[36] The health of the state is dependent on the health of its citizens, just as the overall health of the body is dependent on the health of its individual members. The ultimate goal, though, is the well-being of the whole organism, not of the individuals or subgroups of which it is constituted.[37] The supreme importance of education is therefore not merely that by it individuals are turned toward the good. Rather it is that as individual citizens are turned toward the good the state, as a collective entity, also becomes good. Plato therefore writes that the government should seek to foster as much wisdom as possible in its citizens, for it is the spiritual folly of the soul, not any ignorance in the realm of the professions, that is most fatal to the well-being of the state.[38]

Before moving on to particulars of the curriculum and pedagogy advocated by Plato, it is necessary to address two key aspects of how he understands education to take place. The first, which pertains primarily to learning, is known as the theory of recollection. The second, which pertains primarily to teaching, is the idea of education as conversion.[39] According to Plato's theory of recollection, learning is not a matter of acquiring new information but rather of remembering what one's soul already knows. The soul, Plato argues, is immortal and moves back and forth between our world and the underworld. When a person is born the soul enters a body, and when the person dies the soul leaves. Because it has existed forever, however, the soul already has encountered

36. Drever, *Greek Education*, 75. Cf. Gabriel Moran, *Speaking of Teaching: Lessons from History* (Lanham, MD: Rowman & Littlefield, 2008), 15: "It has to be constantly kept in mind that Plato views the education of the individual as penultimate to the formation of the perfect community."

37. See, for example, Plato, *Republic* 519e1–520a3. Cf. ibid., 420b3–421c4 and 462a2–e2.

38. Plato, *Laws* 688e3–689c2.

39. Of course both the theory of recollection and the idea of education as conversion have implications for learning as well as for teaching, given the interplay that happens in education between the teacher and the learner.

all knowledge, both in this world and in the underworld. Thus there is nothing that anyone needs to "learn" in the traditional sense, for there is no knowledge that a person does not already possess. What we typically call "learning" is therefore not the process of gaining new knowledge but rather that of recollecting knowledge that is already within us. As Plato explains in the *Meno*:

> As the soul is immortal, has been born often and has seen all things here and in the underworld, there is nothing which it has not learned; so it is in no way surprising that it can recollect the things it knew before, both about virtue and other things. As the whole of nature is akin, and the soul has learned everything, nothing prevents a man, after recalling one thing only—a process men call learning—discovering everything else for himself, if he is brave and does not tire of the search, for searching and learning are, as a whole, recollection.[40]

In the *Phaedo* Plato similarly defines learning as "the recovery of our own knowledge" and argues that, "Those who later, we say, are learning, are only recollecting, and learning [is] recollection."[41]

Education for Plato is not primarily a matter of technical training but rather one of moral formation.

Plato's theory of recollection has obvious implications for how he conceives not only of learning but of teaching as well. Given that students already have all knowledge within them, the teacher's job cannot be to fill their minds with new information. As Plato argues

40. Plato, *Meno* 81c4–d5.

41. Plato, *Phaedo* 75e5; 76a5–6. See ibid., 72e2–77a5 for a more extended version of the theory of recollection.

in his explanation of the famous allegory of the cave, "Education isn't what some people declare it to be, namely, putting knowledge into souls that lack it, like putting sight into blind eyes."[42] Students already have the knowledge within them, as well as the power to learn. What they need is for the teacher to help draw out the knowledge that already is within them. This occurs by means of a conversion experience in which students recollect the knowledge already in their souls by turning from the shadows of this world to the form of the good. This turning is a kind of conversion in that the entire soul is changed.[43] As Plato explains, "The instrument with which each learns is like an eye that cannot be turned around from darkness to light without turning the whole body. This instrument cannot be turned around from that which is coming into being without turning the whole soul until it is able to study that which is and the brightest thing that is, namely, the one we call the good."[44] Given this view of education as conversion, the role of the teacher is to help bring such a conversion about. Teaching therefore does not consist in transferring new knowledge to students or in equipping them with the power to learn. Rather the teacher's goal is to facilitate their educational conversion. According to Plato the teacher's craft, the craft of education, is "the craft concerned with doing this very thing, this turning around, and with how the soul can most easily and effectively be made to do it. It isn't the craft of putting sight into the soul. Education takes for granted that sight is there but that it isn't turned the right way or looking where it ought to look, and tries to redirect it appropriately."[45]

42. Plato, *Republic* 518b5–c1.

43. See Jaeger, *Paideia*, 2:295: "The essence of philosophical education is 'conversion,' which literally means 'turning round.' 'Conversion' is a specific term of Platonic *paideia*, and indeed an epoch-making one. It means more specifically the wheeling round of the 'whole soul' toward the light of the Idea of Good, the divine origin of the universe."

44. Plato, *Republic* 518c4–d1.

45. Ibid., 518d3–7. Cf. C. D. C. Reeve, "Introduction," in *Republic*, trans. G. M. A. Grube (Indianapolis: Hackett, 1992), xvi: "Plato believes that the fundamental goal of education is not to put knowledge into people's souls but to change their desires, thereby turning them around from the pursuit of what they falsely believe to be happiness to the pursuit

To summarize Plato's understanding of the nature and purpose of education, then, we can say that he is not a relativist with regard to either truth or morality. His view of education is focused on the end or purpose of the educational enterprise, and for Plato that goal is the formation of citizens who exhibit harmonious goodness and beauty. Thus education for Plato is not primarily a matter of technical training but rather one of moral formation. The primary purpose of studying the various disciplines is therefore not one of knowledge acquisition or technical training but rather the formation of a well-ordered holistic individual. The purpose of education, however, does not end with the formation of such individuals. Rather education's ultimate purpose is to form well-ordered individuals in order that they might together constitute a well-ordered state. Finally, the theory of recollection and the idea of education as conversion are important aspects of how Plato understands the process of education to take place. With this broad framework in place, we now turn to some curricular and pedagogical distinctives of Plato's proposed model of education.

of true happiness." For a fuller treatment of the Platonic epistemology that undergirds this view of education, see my "An Argument against Sight-lovers: Knowledge and Belief in *Republic* V," in *Philosophy of Education 2007*, ed. Nicholas C. Burbules, 236–244 (Urbana: Philosophy of Education Society, 2007).

Chapter Five
Plato's Model of Education: Curriculum and Pedagogy

While statements about education can be found throughout many of Plato's works, the most extensive proposal for a program of education comes in his most famous work, the *Republic*.[1] In order to make sense of Plato's proposal in the *Republic*, however, it is first necessary to understand the overall structure of the work and the context of sociopolitical arguments within which education is discussed. The fundamental driving question of the *Republic* is "What is justice?" At the beginning of the dialogue a number of definitions are offered by Socrates's interlocutors, but Socrates shows them all to be inadequate. Socrates then proposes that instead of asking what makes an individual just they examine what makes a city just. In explaining his rationale for this shift, he points out that it is easier to read larger letters than smaller ones. Since a city is larger than a single man, he reasons, perhaps justice can be more easily seen when searched for in the larger entity. He therefore suggests that the participants in the dialogue "first find out what sort of thing justice is in a city and afterwards look for it in the individual, observing the ways in which the smaller is similar to the larger."[2] With this strategy in place, Plato then offers (through the mouth of Socrates) an extensive account of what justice is for a city.

He begins this account by arguing that a city is made up of multiple members, each of whom must fulfill a specific function

1. His later work the *Laws* also offers an extended educational proposal, though there are a number of subtle shifts in that work regarding the content of the curriculum and the ages at which each subject should be studied.

2. Plato, *Republic* 368e8–369a2.

in order for the whole city to function properly. He then notes that since each person is born with different abilities, by their very natures some people are better suited for certain tasks while other people are better suited for other tasks. He further points out that individuals are most likely able to succeed at a given job when they focus all their energies on that single job instead of trying to do multiple ones.[3] With these three claims in place, Plato then argues that there are three natural classes of people within a city, each with a specific role. The first class, the producers, is made up of those whose job it is to produce the goods and services that the city needs. People in this class include farmers, industrial workers, merchants, bankers, etc. The second class, the guardians, is made up of those whose job it is to protect the state against enemies. This includes protection against both external enemies (the job of the military) and internal enemies (the job of the police). The third class, the rulers, is made up of those whose job it is to govern and direct the city. These rulers should be philosopher-kings, thinks Plato, who are both wise and powerful and who have absolute authority over the city.[4]

Having established the distinctions between these three classes, Plato then offers an analysis of each class and of how it should interact with the others. The conclusion is that "Everyone must practice one of the occupations in the city for which he is naturally best suited" and that within the city this "doing one's own work" is the definition of justice.[5] Justice, in other words, is brought about by "the money-making, auxiliary, and guardian classes each [doing] its own work in the city."[6] Injustice, on the other hand, is defined as "meddling and exchange between these three classes."[7] Having established what

3. Ibid., 369b6–370c5.

4. At 414b1–5 there is a terminology change as he renames the guardian class "the auxiliaries" and then refers to the ruling class as "the guardians." Thus there can be an ambiguity in discussions of Plato's classes whether the term "guardians" refers to the second class whose job is protecting or the third class whose job is ruling.

5. Ibid., 433a4–5; 433b3.

6. Ibid., 434c7–8.

7. Ibid., 434b8.

justice is for the city, the conversation transitions back to defining justice for the individual. Plato argues that the analogy between the city and individuals works since individuals, like the city, are composed of three natures or elements. These three natures are the rational part, the spirited (emotional) part, and the appetitive part.[8] Like the guardians in the city, the rational element should rule over the soul. Like the auxiliary class, the spirited element both obeys the rational part and helps it rule over the appetitive element. Like the producing class, the appetitive element is the largest part of the soul, the most insatiable for money, and the most unfit to rule.[9] Given that the same number and kinds of classes exist within the city as elements within the soul of each individual, he concludes that justice for individuals is the same as justice for the city. Thus since "the city was just because each of the three classes in it was doing its own work," it follows that "each one of us in whom each part is doing its own work will himself be just."[10] The overarching question of the dialogue regarding the nature of justice, therefore, has been answered. Justice for the individual occurs when the three elements of the soul are ordered and regulated in an appropriate and harmonious balance with one another.[11]

The analogy between the city and individuals works since individuals, like the city, are composed of three natures or elements.

It is within the context of this discussion concerning the nature of justice that Plato outlines his proposal for a program of education.

---

8. Ibid., 439d3–441c2, for the discussion of these three parts.
9. Ibid., 441e3–442b1.
10. Ibid., 441d7–e1.
11. See ibid., 443d1–e1, where Plato argues that the just individual "does not allow any part of himself to do the work of another part or allow the various classes within him to meddle with each other. He regulates well what is really his own and rules himself. He puts himself in order, is his own friend, and harmonizes the three parts of himself. . . . He binds together those parts and any others there may be in between, and from having been many things he becomes entirely one, moderate and harmonious."

Given that the justice of a *polis* depends greatly upon its system of education, throughout the dialogue Plato develops a detailed analysis of how education in the *polis* should be carried out. Within the just city, he argues, children should be educated according to the class that they will occupy in society. Given that all people are born with different abilities, they are by nature better suited for the work of one of these three classes. It is the job of the rulers to ascertain the natural abilities of each citizen and assign each to one of the classes based on those abilities. Thus as children progress through the various steps of their formal education, they are repeatedly observed and evaluated by the rulers to see whether they have the abilities necessary to continue on to the next level of education or not. By this method each child is placed into the class for which he is most naturally suited.

[Plato] views education as a process that begins in early childhood and continues throughout one's life.

According to Plato's plan for the ideal city, young children stay at home and receive basic early childhood education from their parents. When they reach age ten, however, children then are taken away from their parents and sent out into the country to be raised by the city's educators.[12] The first stage of education, available for everyone, includes music and poetry as well as physical training. All children also receive training in the subjects of the quadrivium (arithmetic, geometry, astronomy, and harmonics). Beginning when they are seventeen or eighteen, they spend two to three years in compulsory

12. Ibid., 540e5–541a3. There is some ambiguity regarding Plato's ideas for early childhood in that earlier in the *Republic* he claims that children will be possessed in common and will not know who their parents are (457c9–d2). He also says that from birth children will be taken by officials and entrusted to the nurses in charge of the rearing pen (460b5–c1). Plato is unclear on how these varied claims are to be harmonized, and it also is at times unclear whether his proposals are meant for all children or only for the children of the ruling class.

physical/military training. At age twenty, some students are chosen based on their performance and perceived potential to continue their education.[13] These honored students continue studying the sciences and also serve an apprenticeship in military service. Ten years later, at age thirty, there is another evaluation to determine which students are fit to continue on to the next level of education.[14] Those selected to continue spend the next five years (ages thirty to thirty-five) mastering the tools of philosophy by studying dialectic.[15] They then spend fifteen years (ages thirty-five to fifty) in public service to the city by occupying various administrative positions.[16] At the age of fifty those who have successfully completed the program of education become rulers. For the rest of their lives they devote the majority of their time to the study of philosophy, though they also take turns ruling the city and training others to be guardians as well.[17]

Before moving on to the pedagogy that Plato advocates for the teaching of this curriculum, there are two points about his program of education that should be emphasized. The first is that he views education as a process that begins in early childhood and continues throughout one's life. His treatment of education begins with a detailed account of the stories that are told to young children,[18] and

---

13. Ibid., 537b8–9.
14. Ibid., 537d1–3.
15. See Plato, *Cratylus* 390c9–10, where Plato defines dialectic as the art of knowing "how to ask and answer questions." Cf. Gabriel Compayré, *The History of Pedagogy*, trans. W. H. Payne (Boston: D. C. Heath, 1899), 32n1: "Dialectic, as used in the *Republic*, is neither philosophy nor logic. I doubt whether it can be considered a subject of instruction at all. It is rather a method or an exercise, the purpose of which is to subject received opinions, formulated knowledge, current beliefs, etc., to a sifting or analysis for the purpose of distinguishing the real from the apparent, the true from the false. The Socratic dialogues are examples of the dialectic method. Dialectic might be defined as the *method of thought proper* or the *discursive reason in act*" (emphasis original).
16. Plato, *Republic* 539e2–540a3.
17. Ibid., 540b1–6.
18. See ibid., 376eff.. Cf. Jennifer Wolfe, *Learning from the Past: Historical Voices in Early Childhood Education* (Mayerthorpe: Piney Branch Press, 2000), 6: "Plato believed that if guardians were to be wise, ethical adults, their earliest experiences would need to reflect the values that were important to society. Children in Athens received their earliest education by being told stories and hearing poetry. To that end, he forbade the use of ancient myths and legends which told the tales of gods in love and at war."

it is not until age fifty that his system of formal education achieves its goal by bringing students to the contemplation of the good.[19] Even once this point is reached, the rulers continue in devotion to their studies for the rest of their lives. Thus Plato conceives of education, like a Kierkegaardian understanding of faith, as a "task for a whole lifetime."[20]

The second point to emphasize is that the social class system of Plato's ideal city is an educational meritocracy. That is to say, class determinations are not based on the class of the child's parents but on the natural abilities of the child as evidenced by his educational performance. The placement of an individual into one of the classes is thus based solely on that individual's constitution and merit, not on the merits of the individual's parents. In contrast to traditional Athenian education, Plato also explicitly includes both males and females in his educational program. He acknowledges that men and women clearly do have very different natures. He argues, however, that these differences are not relevant to who should rule the city any more than being long-haired or bald is relevant to who should be a cobbler. Thus males and females should receive the same education, be assigned to a given class on the same terms, and perform the same duties in society depending on their class assignment.[21] A person's continuing educational opportunities and placement within a societal class are therefore based on the merits of the individual alone irrespective of lineage or gender. This system of education is thus theoretically equitable, though not equal. In other words, not everyone receives the same education, but education is distributed equitably in that the education each one receives corresponds to one's natural abilities.

Having examined Plato's proposal for an educational curriculum (*what* should be taught), we now turn to his understanding of

19. Plato, *Republic* 540a3–6.

20. Søren Kierkegaard [Johannes *de silentio*, pseud.], *Fear and Trembling*, trans. Alastair Hannay, Penguin Classics (London: Penguin Books, 2003), 42.

21. Plato, *Republic* 453b7–457c2; 466c4–d4; 540c3–9.

pedagogy (*how* it is taught). Any analysis of Platonic pedagogy is somewhat difficult because he never offers an extensive treatment of the subject. Nevertheless there are a number of observations about his approach to pedagogy that should be made, particularly with regard to environment, play, imitation, and the Socratic method.

Plato is clear that the environment in which education occurs is of utmost importance and that the teacher therefore should carefully control the educational environment. At one point, for example, he compares young children to animals in a pasture. Like animals that day after day unknowingly receive benefit or harm from the crops on which they graze, children likewise gradually accumulate goodness or evil in their souls from their environment. Plato therefore argues that the craftsmen whose work children regularly encounter must be carefully selected "so that our young people will live in a healthy place and be benefited on all sides, and so that something of those fine works will strike their eyes and ears like a breeze that brings health from a good place, leading them unwittingly, from childhood on, to resemblance, friendship, and harmony with the beauty of reason."[22] In other words, the context in which education takes place is itself part of the education: "As every subject in education plays its part in molding the human being, so do the surroundings in which they are studied."[23] Teachers therefore should be concerned not only with what content is being explicitly studied but with the buildings, music, visual art, and other furnishings by which students are surrounded as they learn.

In addition to the importance of the educational environment, Plato also emphasizes the important role that playing has in how children are taught. He writes, for example, that a person can "never become good unless he played the right games and followed

22. Ibid., 401c5–d2.

23. Richard Livingstone, *Plato and Modern Education*, The Rede Lecture 1944 (Cambridge: Cambridge University Press, 1944), 10.

a fine way of life from early childhood."[24] Thus play should be used proactively as a pedagogical tool. Children's education should not be compulsory, he argues, since "no free person should learn anything like a slave" and "nothing taught by force stays in the soul."[25] He therefore concludes that music, poetry, gymnastics, arithmetic, geometry, astronomy, and harmonics should not be taught by force but should be taught through play. An additional benefit according to Plato is that by teaching these subjects through play teachers are able to assess more accurately children's natural aptitudes.[26] In the *Laws* Plato contends that in addition to the liberal arts, specific occupational skills should be taught through play as well:

> The man who intends to be a good farmer must play at farming, and the man who is to be a good builder must spend his playtime building toy houses; and in each case the teacher must provide miniature tools that copy the real thing. . . . We should try to use the children's games to channel their pleasures and desires towards the activities in which they will have to engage when they are an adult. To sum up, we say that the correct way to bring up and educate a child is to use his playtime to imbue his soul with the greatest possible liking for the occupation in which he will have to be absolutely perfect when he grows up.[27]

According to Plato the use of play is educationally significant not only for the development of the individual student but also for the health and stability of the city. At one point he goes as far as to argue that the games children play should be closely monitored and controlled because the principles and dispositions learned from those

---

24. Plato, *Republic* 558b4–5. Cf. ibid., 425a3–5: "When children play the right games from the beginning and absorb lawfulness from music and poetry, it follows them in everything and fosters their growth."
25. Ibid., 536e1–3.
26. Ibid., 536e5–537a1.
27. Plato, *Laws* 643b7–d4.

games affect later legislation within the city and "determine whether the laws that are passed will survive or not."[28]

In addition to play, Plato advocates for the use of imitation as a pedagogical tool. Imitation is educationally formative, he argues, in that "Imitations practiced from youth become part of nature and settle into habits of gesture, voice, and thought."[29] Given the profound educative effects that imitation has on a person, he insists that children imitate only "what is appropriate for them, namely, people who are courageous, self-controlled, pious, and free, and their actions."[30] Children must not be allowed to imitate, however, slaves doing slavish things or people who quarrel or brag, "lest from enjoying the imitation, they come to enjoy the reality."[31] One of Plato's pedagogical proposals for imitation is that in preparation for military service children should be led into war on horses in order to observe the battle and when it is safe should "be brought close and taste blood, like puppies."[32] By observing and imitating the warriors, children are developed into warriors themselves. Plato thus demonstrates what Werner Jaeger calls a "profound understanding of the truth that imitation (especially continuous imitation) influences the character of the imitator. All imitation means changing one's soul—that is, abandoning its own form for the moment, and assimilating it to the character of the model, whether the model be good or bad."[33]

The final aspect of Plato's approach to pedagogy is the Socratic method. The Socratic method is an approach to inquiry modeled throughout Plato's dialogues as Socrates interacts with various interlocutors. Ascribing the Socratic method to Plato as a pedagogical

28. Ibid., 797a7–8.
29. Plato, *Republic* 395d1–2.
30. Ibid., 395c3–5.
31. Ibid., 395c6.
32. Ibid., 537a5.
33. Werner Jaeger, *Paideia: The Ideals of Greek Culture*, trans. Gilbert Highet (New York: Oxford University Press, 1939–1944), 2:223.

method that he advocates, however, is problematic for two reasons. The first has to do with the ambiguous line between Socrates as a historical person and as a literary figure. The question, in other words, is whether in his dialogues Plato uses the character of Socrates to model how Plato thinks teaching should be done or whether the Socratic method simply reflects how the historical Socrates actually taught. The second complication is that at various points in the dialogues Socrates explicitly claims not to be a teacher and while in the very act of using the Socratic method claims that he is not teaching anything. Thus it may seem odd to interpret the Socratic method as a method of teaching at all. Despite these issues, however, the Socratic method plays a prominent role throughout Plato's writings as the primary pedagogical tool by which Socrates "teaches" the other characters in the dialogues.[34]

The Socratic method, also sometimes called the *maieutic* method, is the process of bringing knowledge to birth by asking questions. Given the theory of recollection, people already possess knowledge of all things and merely need to recollect what they already know. The Socratic method is the way that Socrates helps bring that recollection about: He asks questions and allows others to discover truth by answering the questions themselves. The Socratic method takes place in two stages. In the first (destructive) stage, Socrates raises objections to the opinions of his interlocutor in order to expose those opinions as false, inconsistent, or unsatisfactory.

---

34. With regard to the first complication, there is wide debate among Plato scholars regarding how to distinguish between the historical Socrates and Socrates as he is used by Plato as a literary figure. Many believe that the Socrates of Plato's early dialogues fairly closely represents the historical person, while by what is called Plato's middle period Plato uses Socrates more as a literary figure. This interpretation is controversial, however, and certainly not unanimously held. With regard to the second complication, there is again a wide range of interpretation. It is possible to interpret Socrates's denials that he is a teacher as ironic jabs at the Sophists with whom he was at odds, and I have argued elsewhere that when Socrates claims he is not "teaching" he is using the term in a restrictive technical sense. See, for example, my "An Inquiry into Teaching in the *Meno*," *Philosophical Studies in Education* 37 (2007): 143–144. See also Gabriel Moran, *Speaking of Teaching: Lessons from History* (Lanham, MD: Rowman & Littlefield, 2008), 3–5, for a discussion of how various commentators have interpreted Socrates's denial that he is a teacher.

Typically the "student" has given an answer to whatever question is under discussion, and Socrates asks questions in order to help the student realize the problematic nature of that answer. This part of the Socratic method is known as the process of *elenchus*, which means to refute or disprove. Through this process of questioning, the interlocutor is brought to a state of *aporia* ("perplexity" or "confusion") in which he recognizes that he does not know the true answer to the question at hand. Once the student has admitted ignorance, the second (constructive) stage of the process begins. In this stage Socrates searches together with the student for the correct answer to the question by continuing to ask questions and evaluate answers. This process continues until together they discover an answer to the question that can withstand scrutiny by further questions. At this point knowledge has been recollected, and the Socratic method has served its purpose with regard to the particular question at hand.

The Socratic method plays a prominent role throughout Plato's writings as the primary pedagogical tool by which Socrates "teaches" the other characters in the dialogues.

One clear example of the Socratic method occurs in the *Meno* when Socrates attempts to demonstrate the theory of recollection by helping an uneducated slave boy learn (i.e., recollect) a particular geometrical fact.[35] The question concerns the ratio between the legs of two squares if one square has twice the area as the other. The slave boy first answers that since the larger square has twice the area of the smaller one, the length of its legs must be twice as well. Socrates then asks him a series of questions that lead him to admit that this is not true. Having realized that the ratio between the legs of the two squares cannot be 2:4, the boy

35. The slave boy episode in the *Meno* runs from 81e–85b.

then decides that the ratio must be 2:3. By having him calculate the areas of squares with legs of those lengths, Socrates again leads the boy to an admission that his answer is not correct. Finally the boy reaches a state of *aporia* and admits his inability to answer the question: "By Zeus, Socrates, I do not know."[36] Once the boy has admitted ignorance, Socrates then asks him a series of questions to help him see that it is the diagonal of the smaller square that serves as the leg of a square with twice its area. Socrates has successfully brought knowledge to birth by asking questions, and by using the Socratic method he has helped the boy recollect a geometrical fact that his soul already knew.

Thus while Plato never offers an extensive analysis of pedagogy in the same way that he does of his proposed curriculum, it is clear that the learning environment, the use of play, the importance of imitation, and the Socratic method are important aspects of how he thinks education should be practiced. Whatever merits it might possess in its own right, Plato clearly takes the Socratic method to follow from the metaphysical and epistemological assumptions of the theory of recollection. His views on the learning environment, the use of play, and the importance of imitation, however, are not deduced but based on empirical observation, and with regard to these Plato demonstrates remarkable insight into what today would be called educational psychology.

36. Plato, *Meno* 84a2–3.

Chapter Six
Plato's Educational Legacy

It is difficult to underestimate or succinctly capture the extensive and pervasive effects that Plato has had on the history of education. In terms of his own legacy as an educator, the Academy he founded in Athens is generally considered to have been the first fixed European institution of higher learning. It remained in operation for over nine hundred years, from the time Plato opened its doors in the early fourth century BC until it was dissolved by the Emperor Justinian in AD 529 along with the other "pagan schools." Throughout Greece and later Rome, many educational institutions were modeled after the pattern of Plato's Academy. As an educator himself, Plato was responsible for training numerous intellectual and political leaders throughout the Hellenic world. Among the most significant of his pupils were Dion of Syracuse, Python and Heraclides (the liberators of Thrace), Chabrias and Phocion (great Athenian generals), Xenocrates (adviser to Alexander the Great), Euphraios (adviser to Perdiccas III of Macedonia), and Erastus and Coriscus (governors of Assos).[1] The most famous of all Plato's students was Aristotle, who along with Socrates and Plato stands as a central axis of ancient Greek philosophy and a founder of Western thought. Aristotle in turn served as tutor to Alexander the Great, and through Alexander's many conquests the thought of Plato and Aristotle was spread eastward as the process of Hellenization extended throughout Europe and Asia.

1. For more extensive lists of Plato's disciples, see Diogenes Laertius, *Lives of Eminent Philosophers* 3.46–47; H. I. Marrou, *A History of Education in Antiquity*, trans. George Lamb, Wisconsin Studies in Classics (Madison: University of Wisconsin Press, 1982), 64–65.

Even more important than the legacy left by his own work as an educator, however, is the effect that Plato's thinking about education has had on the history of education. Like Alfred North Whitehead's claim about the European philosophical tradition writ large, it can be argued that the Western tradition of educational theory is but a series of footnotes to Plato's thought. His work on education was seminal in that he was the first person in the Western tradition to offer a systematic theory of education. As Frank M. Flanagan explains, "What is of crucial interest in Plato's discussion of education is not the answers he suggests but his identification of the relevant questions and problems in the first instance. Plato was the first to write about education in a systematic and reflective way."[2] Gabriel Compayré similarly refers to Plato's work on education as "the germs of a science of education based on psychology, ethics, and politics."[3] Regardless of whether in various historical epochs his educational ideas were accepted or not, Plato asked the questions that framed educational theory from the fourth century BC onward.

It is in fact the case, however, that throughout history many of Plato's educational ideas were accepted and implemented. Roman educational thought, particularly that of the leading theorists Cicero and Quintilian, was in large part simply a Roman adaptation of the fundamental principles of Platonic education. During the Middle Ages Plato's ideas did not have as direct an effect on the monastery schools and scholastic universities as did those of his student Aristotle, but nevertheless his thought was very much in the background of the education taking place at these institutions. During the Renaissance, however, Plato's thought was a central inspiration for the humanists' views on education, and according to Robert Ulich, since the time of the Renaissance, "All humanist or neo-humanist movements in education have started with the battle cry: 'Back to

2. Frank M. Flanagan, *The Greatest Educators Ever* (London: Continuum, 2006), 22.
3. Gabriel Compayré, *The History of Pedagogy*, trans. W. H. Payne (Boston: D. C. Heath, 1899), 42.

Plato.'"[4] James Drever goes further and argues that Plato's educational theory, or that of Aristotle, who was in large part responding to Plato, laid the presuppositions that underlie the theories of "all educational writers previous to Rousseau, and some after him."[5] For better or worse, Plato's emphases on a liberal view of education as opposed to a utilitarian one, on continuous student evaluation,[6] on the compulsory nature of education, and on the state as ultimately responsible for education instead of parents[7] all have profoundly shaped educational practice for nearly two and a half millennia. Thus in addition to asking the educational questions that have framed the history of educational theory, the answers that Plato gave to those questions have been accepted and further developed by key educational thinkers from ancient Greece to the twenty-first century.

> ***Plato asked the questions that framed educational theory from the fourth century BC onward.***

---

4. Robert Ulich, *History of Educational Thought* (New York: American Book Company, 1945), 23.
5. James Drever, *Greek Education: Its Practice and Principles* (Cambridge: Cambridge University Press, 1912), 3. Drever goes on to argue that even the educational thought of figures such as Jean-Jacques Rousseau, Wilhelm Froebel, and John Dewey look for guidance to the educational theories of Plato and Aristotle.
6. See Marrou, *History of Education in Antiquity*, 75: "The philosophers of the future must be both prepared and at the same time tested: Plato was the first to stress this fact, which has since become a commonplace for all educators."
7. See Compayré, *History of Pedagogy*, 42: "In the *Republic*, we see the theory of compulsion in both its phases: the State must provide an education suitable for State needs; and the young must accept this education because the State has ordained it. For the first time in the history of thought, the State appears distinctly and avowedly as an educator."

Chapter Seven

The Relevance and Implications of Plato's Thought for Twenty-First-Century Education

What, then, does Plato's educational thought have to offer to twenty-first-century education? Certainly much is different in the educational context of the twenty-first century from what it was in Plato's day. Society has changed, human knowledge has greatly expanded, and significant shifts have occurred in our understanding of politics, psychology, and the nature of knowledge. The question, nonetheless, is what insights or correctives Plato's analysis of education within his own context might have for our understanding of education nearly two and a half millennia later. While many answers could be given, perhaps the most beneficial insights come from highlighting key aspects of his thought that stand in stark contrast to prevailing assumptions about education in our current century. To that end, let us revisit three important aspects of Plato's thought and consider how they challenge the assumptions of our contemporary educational milieu.

In the twenty-first century we tend to view formal education as something that needs to be completed quickly as a precursor to the task of living "real life."

The first is that Plato conceives of education, even formal education, as a lifelong process. In the twenty-first century we tend to view formal education as something that needs to be completed quickly as a precursor to the task of living "real life." Children complete their compulsory education before they reach the age of twenty, and after only four more years they can enter society with a college degree that signifies for many the end of their formal education. Even those who go on to do the highest level of graduate work typically exit the system of formal education before they are thirty years old. Especially considering the difference in life expectancy between our age and that of ancient Greece, this stands in stark contrast to Plato's program of formal education that does not reach its climax until the age of fifty. Even once the rulers "graduate" from formal instruction, Plato argues that for the rest of their lives they should devote the majority of their time to academic study. The twentieth-century distinction between formal education and "real life" is furthermore undermined by Plato's proposal for education in that throughout his program there are alternating periods of study and practice. Thus while formal training is a prerequisite for certain jobs within society, for Plato it also is true that practical life skills are a prerequisite for certain types of advanced study. Education and life experience, in other words, are interdependent and cannot be neatly sequenced such that one begins where the other ends.[1]

Second, Plato understands education to be primarily about cultivating people's character, not about equipping them for specific occupational tasks or functions within society. In the twenty-first century, most people assume that the primary purpose of education, if not its only purpose, is to equip students with the knowledge and technical skills that they will need in order to go out into the world and "be successful." The discussion of virtue as the goal of education is strikingly absent, and when "virtue education" is discussed

---

1. See Bernard Bosanquet, *The Education of the Young in the "Republic" of Plato* (Cambridge: Cambridge University Press, 1917), 16. Bosanquet argues that for Plato, "Education is a lifelong process, and has two inseparable sides. You cannot 'complete your studies' at twenty-three or twenty-four, and then, leaving study behind, pass on to practice. The best kind of knowledge—the knowledge of what makes life worth living—cannot be won except by a mind and character trained and matured in the school of life; and again, no good work can be done in the arena of practice unless inspired by the highest spirit of study—the vital enthusiasm for truth and reality."

it is generally treated as an add-on to the curriculum, not as the overarching goal of everything that is studied. Richard Livingstone's trenchant depiction in 1944 of this illiberal approach to education is all the more true of education in the twenty-first century:

> It is characteristic of to-day that, when we discuss which subjects should be studied, or which languages should be learnt, the first consideration is nearly always utility; we ask what is most useful for the machine, not what is most likely to make a good human being. . . . At times, the right motto for our education seems to be *Propter vitam Vivendi perdere causas*: "For the sake of livelihood to lose what makes life worth living." The material in life tends to dominate. . . . Spiritual and moral life is forgotten: wisdom and even judgment recede into the background.[2]

The principal question that must be asked of any educational proposal is not what practical or economic impact it will have but whether it promotes the moral formation of those toward whom it is directed.

This depiction of education was largely true of Athenian education in the Plato's day as well. The Sophists had convinced many Athenians that the measure of educational success was one's ability to win an argument, convince a jury, or please an audience. Plato's critique of this view, as relevant today as it was over 2,400 years ago, is that utilitarian ends such as these are paltry substitutes for the true *telos* of education. The purpose of education is the formation of human beings who are

2. Richard Livingstone, *Plato and Modern Education*, The Rede Lecture 1944 (Cambridge: Cambridge University Press, 1944), 22.

good. Thus the principal question that must be asked of any educational proposal is not what practical or economic impact it will have but whether it promotes the moral formation of those toward whom it is directed. Knowledge without virtue is worse than useless—it is pernicious, and the goal of education is therefore not merely to impart knowledge but also to nurture in students the wisdom necessary in order for that knowledge to be used for the good.[3]

Third and finally, Plato argues vehemently that a system of quality education is essential for the survival of a society. The ultimate goal of his system of education is the cultivation of a virtuous state, and it is to that end that education focuses on the cultivation of virtuous citizens. As Plato explains, "Only if the younger generation has received and goes on receiving a correct education shall we find everything is 'plain sailing,' whereas if not—well, it would be inappropriate to describe the consequences."[4] It is because of this relationship between education and the health of the state that every aspect of a child's education must be so carefully monitored. Even apparently benign activities such as playing children's games and listening to music or poetry must intentionally and diligently be controlled. A proper education in music and poetry is of civic importance, he thinks, because music and poetry have the ability to breed lawlessness that in turn "overthrows everything, public and private."[5] The nature of children's games, which constitute a key component of his early childhood education, similarly determine whether things will go well in the city or

---

3. See Livingstone, *Plato and Modern Education*, 25, for his analysis of why such wisdom is necessary: "Everyone needs a philosophy of life, a sense of values by which to judge and use the gifts of material civilization. . . . We are individualists; without standards to control it, individualism is apt to reveal itself as eccentricity and to end in chaos. We are free; without standards freedom only gives greater latitude of error. Our possessions and opportunities multiply; without standards we have no idea of their relative value, no principle of choice among them, except the whim of the moment." Cf. ibid., 23, where he writes that an age that has knowledge without clear values and beliefs "drifts on the tide of the moment, and in political or economic collapse is the ready victim of . . . anyone with real beliefs, however pernicious, however absurd."
4. Plato, *Laws* 813d3–6.
5. Plato, *Republic* 424e1.

whether it will be "impossible for [children] to grow up into good and law-abiding men."[6] It is because of the direct effect that education has on the welfare of the state that Plato argues those in charge of society "must cling to education and see that it isn't corrupted without their noticing it, guarding it against everything."[7]

Plato recognizes that the health of a society is dependent not merely on the knowledge it possesses but on the values that govern the use of that knowledge.

Within the twenty-first century most would concur with Plato that the survival and health of a society is at least partially a function of the quality of education provided for its citizens. Many assume, however, that the primary benefit of education to society is of an economic nature. For Plato, on the other hand, education's primary benefit to society is not economic but rather its formation of virtuous character: "The character of a people is responsible for its social and political life, [and] education is mainly important because it produces or modifies that character and thus affects the public interests."[8] A society is not served by education because education enables it to prosper economically but because education fosters a character in its citizens that enables them to use whatever prosperity they enjoy for good. As with the health of the individual, Plato recognizes that the health of a society is dependent not merely on the knowledge it possesses but on the values that govern the use of that knowledge. An increase in knowledge alone is of no lasting benefit to society and in fact often leads to nothing but a more elaborate barbarism. Thus for Plato, "The ultimate importance of any nation

6. Ibid., 424e6–525a1.
7. Ibid., 424b3–4.
8. Richard Nettleship, *The Theory of Education in the "Republic" of Plato*, Classics in Education 36 (New York: Teachers College Press, 1968), 45.

is estimated not by its conquests, commerce or comfort but by the values which it has brought in to the world and the degree to which they are embodied in its life."[9]

Plato's understanding of education, then, offers a sharp challenge not only to twenty-first-century assumptions about education but also to our understanding of the role that virtue must play within society if society is to survive. He certainly would have agreed with Samuel Johnson's claim that "No people can be great who have ceased to be virtuous,"[10] and the implications of this claim are just as pressing and profound today as they were in ancient Athens. As Lutz succinctly argues, "One of the most serious and now most urgent questions facing liberal democracy is whether there is a place in it for virtue. We seem to founder for the lack of it and to risk losing the autonomy we cherish by taking direct steps to foster it."[11] In the fourth century BC Plato offered his analysis of education as a corrective to his contemporary Athenian culture. While we may not agree with every aspect of Plato's analysis, the profound questions he raises and the answers he gives to those questions offer a compelling corrective to our own contemporary culture as well.

---

9. Livingstone, *Plato and Modern Education*, 32. Cf. ibid., 27: "States collapse, schemes fail for many reasons: but the commonest and most fatal cause is the weakness of human character."

10. Samuel Johnson, *The Yale Edition of the Works of Samuel Johnson* (New Haven, CT: Yale University Press, 1958–2013), 10:150.

11. Mark J. Lutz, *Socrates' Education to Virtue* (New York: State University of New York Press, 1998), 1.

Bibliography

Adam, James. *"The Vitality of Platonism" and Other Essays*. Cambridge: Cambridge University Press, 1911.

Aristophanes. *The Clouds*. Translated by William Arrowsmith. In *Aristophanes: Three Comedies*, edited by William Arrowsmith. Ann Arbor: The University of Michigan Press, 1969.

Bosanquet, Bernard. *The Education of the Young in the "Republic" of Plato*. Cambridge: Cambridge University Press, 1917.

Compayré, Gabriel. *The History of Pedagogy*. Translated by W. H. Payne. Boston: D. C. Heath, 1899.

Diener, David. "An Argument against Sight-lovers: Knowledge and Belief in *Republic* V." In *Philosophy of Education 2007*, edited by Nicholas C. Burbules, 236–244. Urbana: Philosophy of Education Society, 2007.

———. "An Inquiry into Teaching in the *Meno*." *Philosophical Studies in Education* 37 (2007): 141–150.

Diogenes Laertius. *Lives of Eminent Philosophers*. Translated by R. D. Hicks. 2 vols. Loeb Classical Library. Cambridge, MA: Harvard University Press, 1972.

Drever, James. *Greek Education: Its Practice and Principles*. Cambridge: Cambridge University Press, 1912.

Eby, Frederick, and Charles Flinn Arrowood. *The History and Philosophy of Education Ancient and Medieval*. Prentice-Hall Education Series. New York: Prentice-Hall, 1942.

Flanagan, Frank M. *The Greatest Educators Ever*. London: Continuum, 2006.

Garrison, Jim. *Dewey and Eros: Wisdom and Desire in the Art of Teaching*. Advances in Contemporary Educational Thought Series 19. New York: Teachers College Press, 1997.

Jaeger, Werner. *Paideia: The Ideals of Greek Culture*. Translated by Gilbert Highet. 3 vols. New York: Oxford University Press, 1939–1944.

Jarrett, James. *The Educational Theories of the Sophists*. Classics in Education 39. New York: Teachers College Press, 1969.

Johnson, Samuel. *The Yale Edition of the Works of Samuel Johnson*. 23 vols. New Haven, CT: Yale University Press, 1958–2013.

Kamtekar, Rachana. "Plato on Education and Art." In *The Oxford Handbook of Plato*, edited by Gail Fine, 336–359. Oxford: Oxford University Press, 2008.

Kierkegaard, Søren [Johannes *de silentio*, pseud.]. *Fear and Trembling*. Translated by Alastair Hannay. Penguin Classics. London: Penguin Books, 2003.

Leeson, Spencer. *Christian Education*. London: Longmans, Green, 1947.

Livingstone, Richard. *Plato and Modern Education*. The Rede Lecture 1944. Cambridge: Cambridge University Press, 1944.

Lutz, Mark J. *Socrates' Education to Virtue*. New York: State University of New York Press, 1998.

Marrou, H. I. *A History of Education in Antiquity*. Translated by George Lamb. Wisconsin Studies in Classics. Madison: The University of Wisconsin Press, 1982. First published 1956 by Sheed and Ward.

Moran, Gabriel. *Speaking of Teaching: Lessons from History*. Lanham, MD: Rowman & Littlefield, 2008.

Nettleship, Richard. *The Theory of Education in the "Republic" of Plato*. Classics in Education 36. New York: Teachers College Press, 1968. First published 1906 by The University of Chicago Press.

Pieper, Josef. *Leisure, the Basis of Culture*. Translated by Alexander Dru. Indianapolis: Liberty Fund, 1999. First published 1952 by Pantheon Books.

Plato. *Complete Works*. Edited by John M. Cooper. Indianapolis: Hackett, 1997.

Plutarch. *Greek Lives: A Selection of Nine Greek Lives*. Translated by Robin Waterfield. Oxford World's Classics. Oxford: Oxford University Press, 1998.

Pounds, Ralph L. *The Development of Education in Western Culture*. New York: Appleton-Century-Crofts, 1968.

Reeve, C. D. C. "Introduction." In *Republic*, by Plato, translated by G. M. A. Grube, viii–xviii. Indianapolis: Hackett, 1992.

Rousseau, Jean-Jacques. *Émile*. Translated by Barbara Foxley. The Everyman Library. London: Everyman, 1993.

Schofield, Malcolm. "Plato in His Time and Place." In *The Oxford Handbook of Plato*, edited by Gail Fine, 36–62. Oxford: Oxford University Press, 2008.

Scolnicov, Samuel. *Plato's Metaphysics of Education*. London: Routledge, 1988.

Thucydides. *The History of Thucydides*. Translated by Benjamin Jowett. 3 vols. New York: The Tandy-Thomas Company, 1909.

Ulich, Robert. *History of Educational Thought*. New York: American Book Company, 1945.

Whitehead, Alfred North. *Process and Reality: An Essay in Cosmology*. Gifford Lectures Delivered in the University of Edinburgh During the Session 1927–1928. New York: The Macmillan Company, 1929.

Wolfe, Jennifer. *Learning from the Past: Historical Voices in Early Childhood Education*. Mayerthorpe: Piney Branch Press, 2000.

Questions for Discussion

1. What are some ways in which Plato's educational thought reflects or is a response to the historical context within which he was working?

2. How were the cultural strengths and weaknesses of Athens similar to or different from those of our own society?

3. Should the primary purpose of education be viewed as developing individuals as holistic human beings or as training them for specific tasks in society?

4. Is the ultimate goal of education the development of the individual? Of the state? Of the church?

5. Is there a legitimate parallel between what justice is for a society and what it is for an individual?

6. How are Plato's views regarding the ideal society similar to or different from contemporary views?

7. What aspects of Plato's thought are reflected in Christian thinking?

8. How are Plato's views regarding the purpose of education the same or different from contemporary conceptions of education?

9. How should we go about determining which stories are educationally appropriate and useful for young children? What restrictions should be placed on the stories to which children are exposed?

10. What aspects of Plato's theory of knowledge are useful for educators to consider? Why?

11. How is Plato's understanding of what it means to be a teacher similar to or different from contemporary conceptions?

12. What aspects of Plato's proposed curriculum are similar to or different from contemporary curricula? In what ways do the curricular differences reflect different conceptions of the nature of human beings or of the purpose of education?

13. In what ways are the assumptions of contemporary educational thought and practice similar to those of Athens during Plato's life? Does our educational system produce "sophists" who are trained to speak persuasively and "succeed" in society but who lack the wisdom and virtue Plato considers so important?

About the Author

David Diener has a BA in Philosophy and Ancient Languages from Wheaton College and an MA in Philosophy, an MS in History and Philosophy of Education, and a dual PhD in Philosophy and Philosophy of Education from Indiana University. He is the Head of School at Grace Academy in Georgetown, TX, and an adjunct philosophy professor at Taylor University. The Dieners have four children and enjoy working, playing, loving, and laughing together.

Notes

Notes

Notes

Notes

GIANTS IN THE HISTORY OF EDUCATION SERIES

C. S. Lewis: An Apologist For Education
Louis Markos, PhD

Plato: The Great Philosopher-Educator
David Diener, PhD

John Milton: Classical Learning and the Progress of Virtue
Grant Horner

"This thoughtful series builds a bridge from the great educational thinkers of the past to the present renewal of classical, liberal arts education."

—Dr. Christopher Perrin

Latin Is Alive!

The Latin Alive! series is a relevant and rigorous introduction to Latin that will make Latin come alive for grades 7–12. Written by experienced and enthusiastic Latin teachers, Latin Alive! is a grammatically based curriculum and illustrates the relevance and power of Latin in history, ancient and contemporary culture, the Romance languages, English derivatives, and the grammatical structure of English. The series features original Latin writings, giving students access to the writing of great Latin authors in their original tongue. Accompanying teacher's editions, which include the entire content of the student edition as well as translations, extensive teacher's notes, and an answer key, are available. Teaching DVDs are also available for books 1–3.

Latin Alive! Book 1

- 36 chapters
- Pronunciation guides
- Thorough grammar explanations including all five noun declensions and cases, all verb conjugations, irregular verbs, various pronouns, adjectives, and adverbs
- Extensive study of the Latin derivatives of English words
- Latin readings and translation exercises
- Roman culture, myths, and history
- Exercises and questions to prepare students for the National Latin Exam and the Advanced

Latin Alive! Book 2

- 33 chapters
- Introduces the passive voice in all tenses; past, present, and future participles; deponent and irregular verbs; comparative and superlative adjectives and adverbs
- Reviews the grammar of *Latin*

Latin Alive! Book 3

- 16 chapters
- Readings include an explanation of the phrases in the reading, a glossary, and comprehension questions
- Unit readings include history about the reading, information on Latin literature (including poetry), and a multiple-choice question section to check comprehension
- More in-depth study of the subjunctive mood, irregular nouns, noun and verb reviews, the gerund and gerundive, impersonal verbs, conditional statements, and a study of different kinds of clauses (purpose, result, doubting, and fearing)

Latin Alive! Reader

- Features 31 fully annotated readings
- Includes writings from authors such as Cicero, St. Patrick, Aquinas, and Newton
- Acquaints students with a broad range of Latin authors and writing styles
- Three veteran Latin educators contributed to the book: Karen Moore, Gaylan Dubose, and

It's Here!
Classical
Teacher Training